They Called Me Eva

There is a copy of this book
in the library of the British Museum
in London, England.
(Of course, they don't know it's there.)

They Called Me Eva

CHRISTINA KAYA

I Saw That!
Toronto

THEY CALLED ME EVA

This edition published by I Saw That!, Toronto, Canada
https://isawthat.com

ISBN 978-0-9219961-8-7

Contents

Prologue

One of my favourite shows is "Finding Your Roots" with Henry Louis Gates. Each week I tune in to learn about the ancestry of celebrities who trace when and where their descendants first arrived in North America.

In my case, I already know. My parents were the first in our family to arrive by ship and settle in Canada, with me in tow. Everyone else in the family lives "back over there". At least, I assume they're over there, in England and Turkey. I am the product of two fallen empires.

On "Finding Your Roots" I hear stories of how family members shun each other, withhold the news of deaths, and go to their graves with secrets. They compete, judge, undermine and belittle each other. They have fights and fallouts over wills.

These are the stories of my family, too. In so many ways we live the same lives, cry the same tears, and share the same pain.

I hope this book makes you laugh.

I think we've all done enough crying.

The Idiot

We were all crammed into a packed plane waiting for take-off to Miami. We didn't know what was causing the delay. A flight attendant walked down the aisle, doing a head count. Later, another passing required us all to show our boarding passes. More delay. Then they started making announcements that were unintelligible. I didn't really pay attention.

At this point I started thinking, "Who is the @#* idiot causing this delay? Why can't people get to the airport on time? People are so stupid. I bet they'll have to take some idiot's luggage out of the hold. Why can't people be organized? People are so #@!!* incompetent."

After about 45 minutes I was getting very impatient, very hot, and quite frankly, very bored. I had finished the newspaper from cover to cover and had read the entire onboard magazine, learning more about some celebrity starlets than I was ever to care less about. Let's get this show on the road! The attendants at the front were still on the microphone, so I wiped the sweat from my brow and started paying attention.

Approximately seven and a half seconds later, my stomach turned over inside of me and a rush of blood flooded my face. Like a bolt of lightning, I realized they were paging "EVA somebody". Although Eva is my first name, nobody has ever called me that. I have only ever been called by my middle name … Christina or Chris, but never Eva. I don't respond to the name Eva. Nobody can ever pronounce my full surname, so it is always unintelligible. But it suddenly registered in my mind that they were paging ME.

I was the !@%$#%@ idiot.

I happened to be sitting at the back near the washrooms, so I had to gather my things and walk up the long aisle of shame, apologizing profusely to everyone on the way. There had indeed been a mistake by the agent at the check-in counter, but these people didn't care that this wasn't my fault. All they knew was that I was the idiot that had delayed their enjoyment of sitting on a beach with a margarita.

Evita

Apparently, I was named after Eva Peron, suggested by my father's best friend at the time, who was from Argentina. Or so they say. I do remember an old black and white photo of my dad with another dark, handsome man, with me between them, holding a dolly, so maybe it was true.

The doll's name was Jacqueline, I remember, and for some reason, all her hair fell out, which upset me greatly. I was so upset that I didn't want another doll after that, preferring instead to have stuffed animals who, even with a bad bout of psoriasis, would still have lots of hair left, even if it was blue.

Panda was my favourite, but one Halloween I threw up all over my beloved bear and that, unfortunately, was the end of Panda. I don't remember playing with dolls or stuffed animals after that.

Anyway, having Eva as my legal first name and being called something completely different would turn out to be a nuisance at best and a problem at worst. Also, I have often wondered, can I really be summed up by three letters?

Now, if you happen to be named Amy, Ann, Ali, Dan, Hal, Ida, Jim, Joe, Jan, Leo, Lee, Lou, Max, Mel, Rex, Roy, Sid, Ted, Tod, or Tim, please don't get upset with me. Many notable people have had names with three letters. Of course, there was my beloved uncle, Tom. Then there's Roy ... Rogers, Orbison, Schubert.... Many stellar women were named Eva. Eva Peron, Eva Gabor, Eva Longoria, Little Eva....

Then there was Eva Tanguay. Few people know of her. The Queen of Vaudeville, she out-earned Enrico Caruso and Harry Houdini at the time. Her life is portrayed in a movie, *I Don't Care*, starring Mitzi Gaynor.

If you're younger than a certain age, you're probably wondering, "Who is Mitzi Gaynor?" Check out her movies. She is *fabulous*!

Baby Names

It took a month to name each of our children. It upset many folks that these little people were subjected to going a whole month living on earth being called "the baby". Like they knew the difference? But I feel naming a child is a very important decision.

Although I had been mulling over the book of *100,000 Baby Names and Their Meanings* from the moment I found out I was expecting, I had to get to *know* this person before bestowing a name they would have to live with for the rest of their lives.

After all it's not just a baby name. It also must serve them well as a teenage name, adult name, middle-age name, and old-age name. While "Junior" or "Bambi" may be cute for a baby, it might not suit someone who needs to introduce themselves as a lawyer, doctor, carpenter, electrician, dentist, plumber, or someone who generally needs to inspire confidence.

Not everyone likes their name. You would be surprised at how many people change their name. Many people you and I know go by something other than what's on their birth certificate.

Maybe there should be courses on branding as well as breast-feeding.

What's in a Name?

I'm pretty sure my middle name, "Christina" was bestowed by my Grandmother Florence. My early years were spent with Grandma and Grandad in a London rooming house full of international boarders, Lex the dog and five Siamese cats. I would have breakfast on Grandad's knee—kippers, eggs, bangers, and black pudding. The house always smelled of something good cooking in the kitchen.

Grandma Florence was from Yorkshire and lived through WWI, the pandemic of 1918, WWII, and the swinging sixties. She was strong, kind, fair and the eldest daughter of thirteen children. She was a fantastic cook and started her own catering business in the 1920s, which is how she was able to eventually buy a house in London, near West Kensington and Earls Court tube stations. She didn't have her first child, my Uncle Tom, until she was thirty-three years old ... unusual for a woman of her generation.

Grandad Thomas, who was from Newcastle, worked in the coal mines in the north. I remember he really struggled to breathe. He adored my grandmother referring to her as "my Florrie". Grandad was *very* funny. He told stories that would curl your toes. He taught me the army's rendition of all the children's nursery rhymes.

I have always liked my name. Apart from being nine letters, Christina has been a useful name because of its flexibility. Back in the olden days before everybody was equal, I entered essay contests with the name "Chris" as it was gender neutral. It gave me great pleasure to see surprised expressions when I showed up to collect my prize.

It's often good to do something unexpected.

Euphemisms

My early childhood at 63 Castletown Road was a happy one. We would all sit in the main room, which had a fireplace, the only source of heat in the house. It was a wonderful gathering place where I would play records of *Peter Rabbit* and *South Pacific* on the record player. Whether they liked it or not, everyone got to listen to me sing "Dites-moi" and "Happy Talk" many, many times.

I slept in the very top room of the house with the five Siamese cats and three hot water bottles. I remember the sheets were always damp.

Boarders came and went, but I got to know the long-term tenants. There was Jillian and her mother from Jamaica. I recently came across an old black and white photo of us in a park, probably Normand Park, on one of those rare sunny days.

There was Joe and his brother from Malta. At least I assumed they were brothers. They were always so nice and funny, and brought me sweets.

Then there was Mr. Baykal, who only had one leg and got around on crutches. Everyone said Mr. Baykal had "lost" his leg in the war. I remember everyone breaking into laughter when I said "I don't think Mr. Baykal is ever going to find his leg because he didn't lose it. It was blown off." I don't know—is that funny?

Years later in Canada my parents and little brother and I came across a bird in Edwards Gardens that only had one leg. My father, being Turkish with somewhat limited English at the time, referred to it as the bird with the "broken leg". We took it back to the apartment and nursed it back to health on the balcony until it could fly.

At the end of that summer, I was horrified when the phone rang and we learned that my teacher had a broken leg. I had visions of showing up at school and seeing her "missing" a leg, just like Mr. Baykal and the bird. I was *so* relieved when I saw the cast.

There's a difference between "lost", "missing" and "broken", although sometimes people can be all three.

Sort of like "copy", "emulate" and "mock". And when someone says they're "fine", they probably don't mean they're "slim" or "thin". In fact, it could often be more accurate to say they're "thick" … which could mean "wide" or "chunky" or "stupid".

Where's the Pig?

After a couple of days working in western Canada, I got home on a late flight and walked into a dark house. Everyone was asleep. The girls were in bunk beds at that time. When I crept into their room to watch them sleeping, my youngest sat up abruptly and asked, with great excitement, "Where's the pig?"

She had been dreaming, of course, and I attempted to settle her down to return to her slumber. However, she insisted that I *must* have a pig. Finally, I asked her: "What makes you think I would have a pig?"

She replied, "You said you were going to win a pig."

(Winnipeg, if you haven't already figured it out.)

Lucky

Have you ever thought about how …

… if you happened to be born a pig …

… you would be a very lucky pig …

… if you happened to be born ...

... in Israel?

I have.

That Sinking Feeling

When my eldest daughter was all grown up, she told me that something had traumatized her as a child.

My heart sank.

Any parent would feel panicked, as did I. My mind jumped to worst case scenarios.

A predatory neighbour we didn't know about?

A school bully?

She explained: "Whenever you took the train to Montreal to work, everybody was saying that Quebec might separate. I was scared that if they got separated while you were there, and it floated out into the ocean, that you wouldn't be able to get back home."

And my heart sank.

Of course, when she was in her teens she wouldn't care less if I got lost on a slow boat to China.

Forget saving for college. Save to send your teenager to a boarding school in a very faraway country so they become someone else's problem ... but just for a while.

Because all too soon, they grow up and move out and move away.

And your heart sinks.

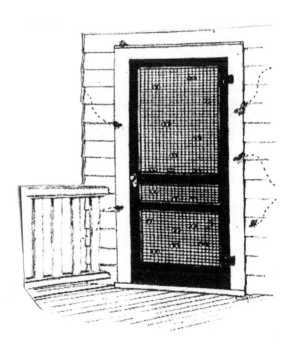

Inside Out

One summer when my youngest was five, she was making mud castles in the backyard with her friends. Needing a constant supply of water, she was going in and out of the kitchen, leaving the screen door open often enough that soon the kitchen was full of flies.

Finally, I stopped her on one of her trips and said, "Please close the screen door behind you. You're letting flies into the kitchen."

She looked up at me with that impish smile and said:

"Well, I'm letting them out."

That's my girl.

The Devil is in the Details

Shortly after we immigrated here my teacher asked the class, "What does your father do for a living?"

I answered, "He's a … communist?"

He was actually an economist.

It was the sixties, so it took a while for those shock waves to come to shore.

Hindsight

The evidence of being a good parent is that your children grow up to afford their own psychiatrist.

I guess that means my parents were successful.

Murder?

Growing up in apartments, we were not allowed to have pets.

Of course, there was that one time we secretly got two "female" hamsters that had fourteen offspring. Many of them escaped into the bowels of the building. Soon there were reports of an infestation of "mice".

Now most of the mice I know are grey and tiny. Hammy was blonde and Chippy was a motley mix of dark brown and taffy markings. None of the kids were grey. Also, hamsters are much larger, so I don't know what those tenants were smoking. Most people smoked in those days.

I hoped none of the kids got caught in a mouse trap, which must be very painful, but I'm afraid many probably did. I try not to think about that.

Anyway, at the height of the extended hamster family, before "the great escape", we kept them in the bathtub most of the time, so they had space to run around. During building inspections, we would keep the bathroom door shut. When the inspector was in the far bedroom, we'd move them to the bedroom that had already been inspected. Musical chairs, only with bedrooms ... and hamsters.

On occasion, the inspector did mention an odd smell, to which my mother would reply, in her best British dialect, "Yes, you should really look into that."

The almost murder happened the year our class iguana had nowhere to go for the Christmas holidays. Seizing the opportunity to have a pet, even if only for two weeks,

I said "it" could come home with me. I don't remember its name and I don't think anyone knew its sex, but when it comes to reptiles … who knows? Come to think of it, we could have given it an androgynous name, like "Chris".

Anyway, on the last day of school before the holiday break I was sent home with the iguana in a glass aquarium with great anticipation of my mother's surprise when I showed up with "Chris".

The one thing I hadn't anticipated was the weather. It was about 30 degrees below zero that day. By the time I reached the lobby of the apartment my hands were freezing, my feet were freezing, and so was "Chris", who at this point was lying grey and comatose on the floor of the aquarium. I had killed the class iguana.

I burst into tears and buzzed to be let into the building. I must have sounded hysterical because by the time the elevator doors parted on the fourth floor my mother was standing there, panicked about what had happened to make me so upset.

In hindsight, her seeing that I was OK must have softened the blow of learning about our hosting "Chris" for the holidays.

As it turns out, when iguanas are cold, they turn grey and comatose. When they warm up, they go back to being green and awaken. After about a half hour by the radiator, "Chris" was OK and I was relieved that I did not, in fact, murder the class iguana.

If the walk home from school had been five minutes longer.…

Important Advice

Don't ever reveal who is in your will.

It gives someone the incentive to knock you off.

Especially if they think you're rich.

Company Policy

My mother loved to host dinner parties. Dad, not so much. He was also known for doing things that were unexpected.

At a certain point in the evening, we children were sent upstairs to bed, just like in *The Sound of Music*, except without the performance of "So Long, Farewell".

But we never fell asleep. In our darkened rooms we listened to the muffled conversations and laughter in the glow of downstairs.

One thing was never muffled. When guests had worn out their welcome my dad would announce, in his loud, Turkish voice:

"Well, I better go to bed now, so these people can leave." Then he did.

Then we would hear his feet on the stairs.

Then everybody went home.

Then we would fall asleep.

In that order.

Lost in Translation

Turkey is known for its beautiful, painted wooden spoons. My mother was in Izmir's market one day and saw some, so she approached the vendor standing behind the counter. Now, if you're tall, blonde, and British, you tend to stand out in a Turkish market. Mom didn't look Turkish, didn't sound Turkish and acted in a decidedly British manner. In her best broken Turkish, she asked the vendor to show her the spoons on the counter. The vendor went pale and took a step back.

Naturally, when a foreigner doesn't understand you, you just need to repeat the phrase, only LOUDER. However, this didn't seem to produce different results. When you've repeated the phrase louder and they still don't understand, then clearly, some additional non-verbal communication is required.

Using her index finger like a jack hammer to indicate the countertop, she said, in Turkish, loudly of course, "I would like to see your spoons."

The vendor looked very upset. Dad was having fits of laughter.

She was actually saying, "I want to see your balls on the counter."

They left without any spoons.

My Friend Pippi

The summer I turned twelve we moved into a house in the suburbs of Toronto. At the end of the street, adjacent to undeveloped wilderness, before the baseball diamond and tennis courts were built, lived a family with six children.

The garden was wild. The house was wild. The children were wild. The eldest was my age and had flaming red hair in pigtails, just like Pippi Longstocking. We fast became friends. We did all sorts of wild things. After years of being cooped up in apartments it was freeing to live in a house, where your connection to the earth didn't involve a ride on an elevator.

Out of all the wild things she taught me, throwing knives was the best. Pippi taught me how to throw knives. In fact, we played "knives". This game couldn't be played today due to laws of safety and the annoyances of parental intervention, but this was an era when laws were lax, and parents didn't really pay much attention to kids. We could go anywhere and do anything we wanted, so long as we showed up before the streetlights came on at dusk.

To this day I know just how to throw a knife so it will stick into anything. Same with axes, but that's another story.

Rocky Ride

The day arrives when you decide you need to follow a longstanding dream. I had seen mine in movies. I had seen it on TV. I had seen it advertised in travel magazines. While I still had some cartilage left in my knees, I was going riding in the Rocky Mountains. On a horse.

I hopped on a plane to Calgary and headed west. Blue skies, bright sunshine and a backdrop of majestic mountains capped with snow. Past the foothills of Alberta, past Canmore, past the hoodoos, I finally arrived at the hotel. Why was I not surprised to see a moose head mounted on the wall in the lobby?

The next day I walked and walked and walked up the mountain road. I kept walking up and up … so far, in fact, I thought for sure that any moment I was going to hear "Ricola!" … "Ricola!" … or I would see Heidi and her grandfather or run into one of the Waltons. A younger person might be wondering, "Who are the Waltons?"

Finally, I reached a long log building with a sign that said, "Riding Stables". It looked just like the picture on the web site. That was a good sign.

The lady behind the counter welcomed me and said: "What kind of experience are you looking for?" I must have heard incorrectly because I answered the question as if it was, "What kind of *horse* are you looking for?"

I thought I wanted a nice horse. An older horse. Maybe a horse with a slight limp. Maybe a bit of a wheeze. One that wasn't going to take off galloping to the edge of a cliff and buck my body into the Bow River.

"What do you suggest?" I asked.

The lady said, "You can take a two-hour trail ride or join us for a full day, which includes a cookout. We catch our own lunch."

So, at this point I'm thinking … are we talking fish, small rodents, or deer? I'm a city girl. I've never actually met my food and there's no way I'm gonna eat Bambi.

I also thought six hours splayed on a horse's back might compromise my ability to walk straight or walk at all for weeks, maybe months. "The two-hour trail ride sounds great." She said I could ride Little Man. Little Man. That was a good sign.

I was led to a line of horses all saddled up, ready to go. I thought about what those horses were probably thinking. Yeah, here's another bunch of city slicker suckers, willing to trust us with them on our backs for what they think is going to be a trail ride. We have the total ability to buck their bodies into the Bow River.

I was relieved to see that as far as horses go, Little Man wasn't too tall. That was a good sign. He seemed relaxed. Also a good sign. He didn't seem competitive in nature so he would likely follow the pack and let the other horses go first. In fact, he seemed so amicable that he probably shared his oats and hay to score points with the other horses, who would give him preferential treatment in the event of a rockslide or an encounter with a bear or cougar, or a moose seeking revenge for his unfortunate cousin, whose head was hanging in the lobby of my hotel.

I was feeling quite good about the whole thing.

I approached from the left, as I had been instructed to do and looked into Little Man's left eye. I had to seem confident. I had to seem like I was in charge. I had to sound authoritative. I firmly patted his neck and said, in the deepest voice I could muster: "Hey there Little Man."

He snorted.

I stepped back.

He stamped a hoof.

I took another step back.

With some help, actually quite a bit of help, actually with the help of a two-and-a-half-foot high step ladder and the strong hands of a strapping young mountain lad, I got into the saddle and was all poised to fulfill my life-long dream.

Little Man and I fast became friends. For the next two hours we walked the mountain trails with breathtaking views and the delicious, fresh, pine scented air. I had never experienced anything like it. And we didn't encounter one moose.

I had fulfilled my lifelong dream.

Would I go again?

In a heartbeat.

I still have some cartilage left in my knees.

One More Time

After returning to Toronto, I called Sunnybrook Stables and booked another trail ride.

My horse's name was Buck.

Really was.

I wonder if Little Man ever thinks of me. I think of him.

In fact, I will remember him always.

The Queen's Plate

In 1979, the Queen Mother attended the running of the Queen's Plate at Woodbine track in Toronto. There were only two people in the stands wearing Derby-style hats: the Queen Mum ... and me.

My date and his father were avid fans of the track. They took great pains to study and handicap the horses to place the best bets. I was excited to be there. I loved horses. And it was the Queen's Plate!

Not being a gambler and really having no idea who might win any given race, I abstained from placing bets. However, after much encouragement and the gift of a five-dollar bill, I thought I'd give it a go.

There was one jockey who had a guitar on his silks. Apparently the owner of the horse had a country music radio station. As I play the guitar, I placed my bet on that horse. The odds were 16:1. My horse came in first and I won a bunch of money. They couldn't believe it.

Sometimes it's just beginner's luck, or maybe serendipity.

Kaya 15

Seeking Serendipity

Serendipity is often portrayed as just luck—an unintended, unexpected combination of events that leads to a wonderful outcome. The translation in most languages is "a happy accident".

Well, I was in a hardware store seeking an electric power drill. The power chain saw that I bought to trim the trees accidentally damaged a wooden fence that was now misaligned and needed to be fixed. A power electric drill was just the tool I needed.

I got in line behind three men who, I noticed, were not purchasing power tools. A smoke detector, a quart of paint ... green I think, and a pack of light bulbs ... just four, I think. I held my power electric drill so everyone could see that I clearly belonged in a Home Hardware. I was feeling good about the whole thing.

While standing in line, some small, orange neon things caught my attention. What were they? Personal flotation devices for children. Kiddie PFDs.

Now, I never learned to swim. The lakes in Canada are far too cold for me and the frigid temperatures of high school swimming pools when I was growing up were obviously regulated by cottage-going Canadians who were used to taking dips in Lake Huron, which isn't too far from Hudson's Bay, which isn't too far from the Arctic Circle.

I believe that in this case, "gym class" is a euphemism for torture. I felt that jumping into a freezing swimming pool to suffer for 45 minutes while the life-guard instructor runs up and down the deck blowing a whistle so hard that it would deafen the dead, was insane.

So, I bought a "personal flotation device" and regularly visited the swimming pool in my apartment building where the water temperature was clearly moderated by immigrants who came from warmer climates.

So, I learned to swim all because my trees needed trimming.

Now, *that's* serendipity!

I Wonder

When someone tells you they have

twenty years of experience …

… does that really mean

twenty years of experience …

OR

… does it actually mean

one year of experience …

… repeated twenty times?

I think it's important to know.

Walkies?

A day without sunshine is … well … night. Steve Martin said this, but I think he lives in California. Younger people may be wondering, "Who is Steve Martin?"

A day without sunshine is par for the course if you live through winter in my part of Canada. You can go weeks and weeks without seeing a lick of sunshine. In fact, living through a Canadian winter is *not* for the faint of heart. If it doesn't kill you, it builds character, if not bring on depression.

However, it's important to get out for a walk. I walk every day. But not if it's raining, sleeting or too windy or too cold. So, maybe not every day. Well, some days. Occasionally. OK—rarely, in the winter, anyway.

However, it's good to get out for a walk after summer sets in, around mid-June, after the snow melts and the mosquitoes have partially died off. Then I walk every day. But not if it's raining or too hot or too humid. So, maybe not every day. Well, some days. Occasionally. OK—rarely, in the summer, anyway.

Then we've got some good days in September. Not too hot, not too cold … then winter kicks in. By November you're back into winter mode. So maybe I don't walk as often as I should.

But I get out when weather permits. So, maybe two or three days a year.

You Can Do It Yourself

The COVID pandemic is well past the one-year mark and without a haircut, I am starting to resemble the Wild Woman of Borneo. When I look in the mirror, what comes to mind is a Tibetan mountain yak or a Jackson Pollock painting.

While I'm thankful to Robert Hinchfield who started mass-producing scissors in 1761, when it comes to the need for a haircut, having a pair of scissors without a hairdresser is like having a slide rule without an engineer. (What's a slide rule?) Like having a rotary dial telephone without someone over the age of 50. (Rotary what?)

As it turns out, I'm not very good at cutting my own hair.

You know, I have a long history of trying to do things I'm not good at. I once bought a dining room set for a really great price. It just had to be assembled.

After three days of putting it together, taking it apart and putting it back together again without following the convoluted instructions, I was proud to have a table and six chairs sitting in my dining room.

However, I also had a large pile of screws and washers left over.

I decided I would just make sure I didn't invite anyone to dinner that weighed more than 150 lbs. Of course, that considerably narrowed down the potential guest list. I could keep a weigh scale at the door to avoid any lawsuits. "If you weigh too much, dine at your own risk."

Then again, the invitations could read "B.Y.O.C." (Bring Your Own Chair).

I ended up giving the dining room set and bag of hardware to my brother.

He's a carpenter. He'll figure it out.

Makes Scents

I *love* the smell of petrol, a.k.a. gasoline. When pumping gas, I have always savoured the aroma of the fumes wafting from the pipe. I never knew why. Then one day it hit me like a barrel of oil.

In the 1960s children were not allowed hospital visits when their siblings were born. I have a clear image of my mother waving from a window up high in a huge grey brick building.

I don't remember anything remarkable about when she brought the baby home except that I wasn't really expecting him to stay.

But he did.

As "mummy's little helper" I remember being part of the diaper changing brigade and fill-ups happened not infrequently. This was before Huggies and Pampers. This was the era of cloth nappies, baby.

It was important to keep little bottoms protected from the harshness of the industrial strength cotton that was required to do the job, so Vaseline was applied liberally at every changing. The answer to my quirky predilection for gasoline fumes lies in that early experience. Vaseline is petroleum jelly!

In those days, petroleum jelly smelled like gasoline. So, for me, the smell is an olfactory sense memory of being mummy's little helper while changing my little brother's diaper.

The baby.

The one who never left.

Makes No Sense

In the '60s you didn't have all the paraphernalia that goes with today's babies. There was no change table. Diaper changes took place on the bed.

Now personally, I'm not sure I would trust a four-year-old with too much responsibility, but my mother did.

One day when my mother left the room, my little brother chose that moment to discover that he could roll over. But it's often good to do something unexpected.

Well, he rolled right off the bed. I suppose it was a good thing he wasn't on a change table or there would have been a longer drop.

For years, my brother accused me of letting him roll off the bed.

For years, I thought he was just joking.

For years, I was mistaken in thinking he was just joking.

He really does blame me for letting him fall off the bed, sometime in 1961.

My mother had told me to "watch the baby", so I watched the baby.

I watched the baby roll right off the bed.

I did exactly as I had been told.

It just makes sense.

One day it will make sense to him.

He's a carpenter. He'll figure it out.

Reconciliation

I know for a fact that I cannot run a marathon.

I tried once, on one very, very deluded occasion.

Puzzling

I know for a fact that I cannot assemble a 1000-piece jig-saw puzzle.

I tried once, on one very, very lonely occasion.

Distilled

During a visit to The World's Largest Bookstore in Portland, Oregon, a good doctor friend of mine conducted an intervention lest I put one more book into my basket. Alas, I live just a few blocks away from a very large bookstore. Despite my attempts to resist temptation I often find myself in Indigo's "just to look".

I came across a *New York Times* bestseller, *The Organized Mind—Thinking Straight in the Age of Information Overload*. I thought this would be something useful for me to read, so despite the doctor's advice, I picked it up and leafed through.

I wondered if it was lost on anyone that this book about distilling information to get organized was 483 pages long. I wondered if it could be rewritten into a more palatable, say, 200 pages? Or better yet, 90 pages?

But then they wouldn't be able to charge $35.00 … or would they? Is a 483-page book more valuable than a 90-page book? Am I paying for quantity or utility? If time is money, perhaps a 90-page book is worth more than a 483-page book.

A couple of weeks later I saw the book beckoning me from a sales table. It was only $15.00. The temptation was too great. I relapsed and bought it.

I'm glad I did. This book provides valuable insights into how we assimilate and process information and practical advice on getting organized.

I think I should probably read it again.

If I can find it.

Less is More

Many years ago, I corresponded with Dr. "Tuzie" Divinsky, Head of Mathematics at the University of British Columbia. He was a chess master and husband to the first (and only) female Prime Minister of Canada.

He also hosted an annual production of Gilbert & Sullivan at the faculty club. (Anyone who is under the age of 90 and doesn't have a British connection is probably wondering, "Who's G & S?")

After I moved back east, his occasional letters were always one page in length. On one occasion his letter was three pages. He signed off with a well-known sentiment:

"Excuse the lengthy letter. I didn't have time to write a short one."

Logical

I was invited for an evening of dinner and Pictionary with neighbours. They are a family of four with two young daughters, a dog named Dharma, and Fred, the cat.

I thought the game was a bit too advanced for the children ... it certainly was for me. Pictionary and most jigsaw puzzles are too complicated for me.

In conversation we got talking about all the different things you can order on Amazon. Dad said that last summer they ordered a dolly that came from Wales. I thought the "dolly" he meant was the kind you dress up and play with, but I knew he meant the country, Wales. The little girl knew he meant the dolly they ordered to carry stuff around in their backyard, but she thought he was talking about "whales".

I wondered why a Welsh doll would be ordered to immigrate all the way over here, when a qualified local doll could probably fill the job.

The little girl wondered why a dolly would be brought here by whales, when you could probably pick one up at the local Home Hardware.

Our misinterpretations were completely logical, really.

We eventually sorted it out.

The lasagna was delicious.

Secrets

It has never, ever occurred to me to look in someone else's medicine cabinet. When I'm a guest in someone's bathroom the only thing I confess to looking for is the cleanest-looking hand towel.

Now, because people apparently do open other people's medicine cabinets, I certainly would not keep things like fungal cream or anti-psychotic pills there because it's the type of thing that's best kept a secret.

Where would I find a selected hiding place for something I wanted to keep a secret? For example, with anti-psychotic pills, I would choose to keep them at the bottom of my sock drawer, in which case the only way a guest would find them is if they had a foot fetish that drew them to explore my sock drawer. Then it wouldn't really matter if they found the pills because in comparison, they would clearly have a more serious problem than I, so they wouldn't mention it.

Keeping your pills in the medicine cabinet is as futile as keeping your booze in the liquor cabinet. If you really want to hide your booze you need to put it somewhere unusual. Some place people are unlikely to look … like behind a book in the bookcase … or under the seat cushion of a chair … or in the hem of a curtain … or in the umbrella stand … or behind a large plant in a large plant pot … or in the hollow space in the vacuum cleaner when the dirt bag is empty … or buried under an extra-deep layer of that granular stuff in your kitty litter box … or in an empty box of Cheerios next to a full box of Wheaties … or inside the hollow box of Lean Cuisine in the freezer … or taped to the back of the television set … or in the water chamber of your toilet....

But definitely *not* in the liquor cabinet.

Not a good place to hide a secret.

The Expen$e of Religion

Life is expensive. Food, shelter, housing … even religion.

Getting to church by transit each Sunday in Toronto costs $6.50 round trip. If you attend regularly this adds up to $338.00 per year. If you sing in the choir and practice on Thursday evenings the cost of going to church comes to $676.00. That's before they've passed that silver collection plate for a fiver.

In Canada the lowest paper denomination is $5.00. You can't get away with throwing in a loonie or toonie because it goes "ka-ching!" … as in "cheap".

In fact, I think they use highly resonant metal on purpose to let everyone in the congregation know who threw in a coin. Some of those collection plates are so resonant you might as well be ringing a bell. Thank goodness (and the Lord) for those little donation envelopes.

Anyway … now I walk to the synagogue around the corner.

The only plate they pass around is the one with the gefilte fish.

And it's free.

Shalom.

Flushed

Aunt Betty's sprawling Caledon estate had all the charms of what was then farm country. A lake with weeping willow trees on sweeping banks, ponies in neighbouring fields and an abundant garden full of herbs, rhubarb, and root vegetables. I remember digging to discover potatoes in the soil for the first time. Before that, I had only known them to come in bags at the grocery store.

The ground floor of the Tudor style house was well-appointed, with antique furniture and a wood paneled country kitchen. The guest bedroom had yellow floral curtains and a matching bedspread. Next to this room was the guest bathroom. This is where the event was going to happen.

Aunt Betty lived a private life. She had never married. I had heard she was at one time engaged to a naval officer but had lost her betrothed in WWII. She never spoke of it, and I never asked. When shopping or travelling, she would dress impeccably in a suit, hat, and white gloves. The world was required to address her as "Miss Sherman". I was allowed to call her "Aunt Betty".

For some reason I had been the chosen one of my siblings and other young people in her life, to spend occasional weekends at her home. While there, I was always on my best behaviour and kept my voice down to the level of a polite hush, lest I disturb the orderly silence of the household. After all, my aunt was from an era when it was believed children should be seen and not heard.

Her only close companion was her cat. He was an enormous grey tabby of the country variety. This cat could swipe a chunk of flesh out of your leg if you went too close, so I didn't. He was a ferocious feline, despite his name, Twink. Short for Twinkle, as in, could murder you in the twinkle of an eye. I always locked my bedroom door at night so he couldn't ambush me in my sleep. I was afraid of that cat.

We would often take afternoon tea in the garden by the lake. On one occasion I took delight in secretly dropping a hefty hit of catnip to Twink. The cat went berserk. He ran in circles, climbed up the rose trellis to the roof and eventually jumped off, landing feet first in the bushes below. It was great. Aunt Betty looked at Twink for some time, bewildered by her companion's unusual behaviour, before declaring in her quiet, proper manner, "Oh, my goodness."

The night the incident happened we had all finished dinner. The other two guests had driven up from the city for the evening. Together we had washed, rinsed dried and put away the dishes, just as they did in the olden days before dishwashers took away that social ritual.

We retired to the living room and took our customary places. Betty sat in her wingback green chair, I in the rose, and the guests on the striped beige and white couch, situated below the large oil painting of a white naval ship on a vast blue ocean. The conversation had turned decidedly boring, at least to me. There seemed to be long spaces of deafening silence. In fact, acres of absolute country silence through which one could drive a tractor. This was a moment that required sherry.

Aunt Betty kept an abundant supply of sherry in the kitchen. The bottles were kept in a floor level cupboard below the display of special plates and crystalware, including some small, elegant sherry glasses. The mugs were kept above the sink. I reached up, opened the cupboard, and got a large one, keeping an eye on the doorway from the living room. I took the mug over to the stash of sherry, poured myself a hefty hit and returned the bottle to the cupboard, keeping an eye on the doorway and another eye out for Twink. That cat had a voice like a wailing wartime siren.

Now I was home free. Holding a mug at the sink with the tap running looked perfectly innocent. I swigged the sherry, rinsed the mug, and returned it to the cupboard. Before re-joining the group I thought I would visit the guest bathroom as the effects of the sherry had loosened my sinuses.

That's when it happened.

Did you know that the tissue you use to blow your nose is quite different than the tissue you use to … well, you know? If you throw Kleenex tissues down a country toilet it can plug the system like an allergy can plug your sinuses. With one fateful flush of the wrong choice of paper, you can clog the toilet and flood the bathroom.

And that's exactly what happened.

I helplessly watched the water circling around and around, higher and higher, spilling over the top of the basin, soaking the rose-coloured carpet under my feet. All I seemed able to do at the time was declare in a quiet but not so proper manner, "Oh, holy sh*t!".

For the first time I noticed a little poem hanging on the wall above the tank:

> "Let me be completely frank.
> Please respect the septic tank."

The sign should have read, in large letters:

"DON'T FLUSH KLEENEX
DOWN THE TOILET!"

The only thing more embarrassing than flooding your own bathroom is flooding someone else's. Especially one that belongs to someone who wears a hat and white gloves to go shopping. In my opinion all Kleenex boxes should be banned from bathrooms. It's far too dangerous to throw temptation in the way of people like me, who lack the ability to interpret elusive poetry.

I looked in the closet for a plunger. There was lots of yellow floral scented soap but nothing useful like a plunger or even a bottle of Drano. Then there was the matter of the carpet. Who has wall-to-wall carpet in a bathroom? It could take days to dry out. Thinking of my options, I looked for a hair dryer. There wasn't one, but the monogrammed towels presented some promise.

I wondered if there was a way to blame it on the cat. Given his earlier demonstration of a tendency towards addiction, I could lock Twink in the bathroom with some of the catnip I had left over. Then the flooded floor would appear in keeping with the shredded shower curtains, soapy canary coloured fur balls and reams of toilet roll paper, criss-crossing the room in patterns reminiscent of a Jackson Pollock painting. But at that moment I had no catnip. And by now, it seemed the cat was avoiding me.

A flood of guilt welled up inside me. The consequences of this flush meant I would have no choice but to confess and that would probably lead to a confession about the catnip and the sherry, and the home-made pie I brought last summer that was actually bought at the farmers' market down the road.

Then there was the time I accidentally knocked the arm off the antique Royal Doulton Blue Boy. I had waited for Aunt Betty's afternoon nap time to roll around. I glued the arm back on, carefully matching the creases in his jacket and put him back on the bookshelf, saluting in the opposite direction to hide evidence of the amputation.

For years now, the grand piano in the library had two white keys stuck together from a piece of toffee I carelessly rested on the end one afternoon and it had melted in the sun. I had never confessed, thinking it was rare that any piece of music required use of the very highest B or C on a piano. That melted confection could be down there forever without detection.

Plus, I had indulged in a secret swig of sherry on more than one occasion.

But now the tide of justice had turned. There was no possibility I would get away with this. Oh, to go back in time to the moment just before I flushed. Suddenly, I wondered how long I had been in there. Maybe I was being missed.

By the time I emerged from the scene of the mishap, the evening was breaking up. If they had wondered about my absence, they didn't reveal it in their faces. The folks signed the guest registry on their way out, as did everyone who visited.

Aunt Betty, feeling tired from a busy day, excused herself and retired for the evening. I surveyed the crime scene one more time and decided the morning would bring the moment of truth and a barrage of confessions.

I went to bed, locking the door behind me.

That night, a huge electrical storm with torrential rain tore through the area. I awoke to a room ankle-deep in water. I waded out to the kitchen, hoping to see the cat, miserable and sopping wet, clinging to safety on the back of a kitchen chair. He wasn't there, but imagining the sight made me smile. It appeared the entire first floor was flooded, including the guest bathroom.

Any need for confession had been washed away.

Betty is now in heaven, so she knows. I'd like to think she has forgiven me for the flood, the sherry, the pie, the piano, the Royal Doulton Blue Boy, and a few other things I haven't mentioned.

But especially for drugging the cat.

Epilogue

No one mentioned in this book is in my life now. Some have passed on, and some have just gone away. While there is so much emphasis on the importance of "family", it is as fragile as a set of valuable glassware. It seems families are easily fractured. If only we handled families as carefully as crystal.

They say that time heals. I'm not so sure about that. I like to think a broken person can be viewed as a repaired Kintsugi bowl. The cracks of gold make the bowl more beautiful than before, even though they are evidence of the bowl having been broken.

Isolation during a pandemic can be particularly difficult for someone with no family. So, I wrote this book. I took up embroidery. I went back to playing my classical guitar. I'm back into magic and mentalism. I re-launched my communications business online, learning that technology has made the world more complicated than I ever dreamt it could be.

I hope this pandemic doesn't last another year, or I may have to write a sequel to this book. I could get a cat and call it "Twink". Or I could become a henna tattoo artist.

It's often good to do something unexpected.

Acknowledgments

Thanks to Joan Bennett and our book club, who introduced me to exploring everything in fiction. Thanks to Jim McAleese, who taught me how to find the funny in everything. And thanks to Ariel, who knows everything.

After a long journey, I am thankful to have found my forever home in the magnificent, magical Thousand Islands. And slowly, I am finding people in my life that are like family to me.

I am grateful for the people in my life who bring me happiness. You may not know who you are, but at the right time, I will tell you.

And I will give you a copy of this book.

9 781777 783020